TURNING POINTS IN US MILITARY HISTORY

D-DAY

Charlie Samuels

Gareth Stevens Publishing

Please visit our website, www.garethstevens.com. For a free color catalog of all our high-quality books, call toll-free 1-800-542-2595 or fax 1-877-542-2596.

Library of Congress Cataloging-in-Publication Data

Samuels, Charlie.
D-Day / by Charlie Samuels.
p. cm. — (Turning points in US military history)
Includes index.
ISBN 978-1-4824-0433-3 (pbk.)
ISBN 978-1-4824-3315-9 (6-pack)
ISBN 978-1-4824-0432-6 (library binding)
1. World War, 1939-1945 — Campaigns — Western Front — Juvenile literature. 2. World War, 1939-1945 — Campaigns — France — Normandy — Juvenile literature. I. Samuels, Charlie, 1961-. II. Title.
D756.5.N6 S26 2014
940.54—dc23

Published in 2014 by
Gareth Stevens Publishing
111 East 14th Street, Suite 349
New York, NY 10003

For Brown Bear Books Ltd:
Editorial Director: Lindsey Lowe
Managing Editor: Tim Cooke
Children's Publisher: Anne O'Daly
Design Manager: Keith Davis
Designer: Lynne Lennon
Picture Manager: Sophie Mortimer
Production Director: Alastair Gourlay

Picture Credits:
Front Cover: Robert Hunt Library.

All images Robert Hunt Library.

Manufactured in the United States of America

CPSIA compliance information: Batch #CW14GS. For further information contact Gareth Stevens, New York, New York at 1-800-542-2595.

CONTENTS

INTRODUCTION

Before dawn on June 6, 1944, the Allies—led by the United States and Britain—launched Operation Overlord, the biggest amphibious attack in history. By nightfall more than 160,000 men would land on five beaches in Normandy in occupied France. Some landings were straightforward. Others faced fierce resistance from the Germans. But everyone knew that if the Allies could at least get a foothold on mainland Europe, then D-Day would be a turning point in World War II.

Long-Term Strategy

D-Day had been years in the planning. Before it could take place, the Allies had to defeat the Germans in other theaters, to draw men away from northern France. Hundreds of thousands of Allied troops had to be assembled, along with the ships to transport them, vehicles, gas, weapons, and ammunition. The Allied air forces had to gain air superiority over the German Luftwaffe. Resistance fighters in France had to destroy German communications.

The coordination involved was remarkable, and the timing of the operation was in doubt until the last minute. On the evening of June 4, the Allied Supreme Commander, US general Dwight D. Eisenhower, studied the weather forecast and made his decision. D-Day would be June 6, 1944.

This view from a landing craft at Omaha Beach shows US troops wading through the surf from their own landing craft.

British reinforcements land on Sword Beach to support the initial assault groups. The Allied soldiers came ashore in a series of waves.

German Mastery of Europe

Before D-Day—June 6, 1944—Germany had controlled most of Europe for nearly three years. At the start of World War II in 1939, its armies rapidly overran its neighbors. Only Great Britain stood between Germany and total domination of the continent. The United States had not yet joined the war, but it sent the British arms and supplies.

German motorcycle troops are on the move in spring 1940. The Germans used vehicles, tanks, and airplanes to make rapid advances.

German Stuka dive-bombers fly in formation to support ground operations. They attacked their targets in a near-vertical dive.

Before 1939 Nazi Germany had used diplomacy to take over Austria and occupy parts of Czechoslovakia. Adolf Hitler, the German leader, had even greater ambitions. On September 1, 1939, Germany invaded Poland. Two days later, Britain and France declared war on Germany. Two weeks later, the Soviet Union also invaded Poland. Germany and the Soviet Union divided the country between themselves.

The Fall of Europe

After a period of inaction known as the phony war, the Nazis invaded Denmark and Norway in April 1940. The next month they took France,

BLITZKRIEG

Blitzkrieg ("lightning war") was a tactic developed by the Germans in the early years of World War II. It relied on rapid advances using Panzer tanks, Stuka dive-bombers, and large numbers of infantry. The Germans stormed through the Low Countries and France in 1940. Once a target was selected, it was bombed from the air and then attacked by tanks and infantry. As the infantry mopped up any remaining resistance, the dive-bombers and Panzers moved straight on to the next target.

Belgium, Luxembourg, and the Netherlands. The British army, which had been sent to protect France, was easily defeated. It had to be rescued from the beaches of Dunkirk.

Britain Fights On

Britain stood alone. The German air force, the Luftwaffe, bombed British cities, and German submarines (U-boats) attacked convoys carrying supplies across the Atlantic. Hitler planned to invade Britain but was unable to destroy the Royal Air Force (RAF). In fall 1940 he decided to plan the invasion of his former ally, the Soviet Union. The same month, Germany, Italy, and Japan formed an alliance, known as the Axis. In October Germany invaded Romania, and Italy entered Greece.

German tanks parade in front of the Arc de Triomphe in Paris after the fall of the French capital in May 1940.

Firefighters try to save burning buildings during the Blitz, the sustained German bombing campaign against London.

BRITAIN STANDS ALONE

In July 1940 Hitler planned to destroy the RAF and then invade Britain across the English Channel. In the Battle of Britain, the Luftwaffe attacked the RAF and its bases for two months. When the RAF survived, the Luftwaffe started the "Blitz." From September 7, 1940, until May 21, 1941, German bombers repeatedly attacked British cities. London suffered most. It was bombed for 57 consecutive nights. Of the 40,000 civilians who died in the Blitz, half were Londoners.

Operation Barbarossa

In early 1941 German troops arrived in North Africa, where their Italian allies were fighting the British, and also invaded Greece. Finally, in June 1941 three million German troops invaded the Soviet Union in what was code-named Operation Barbarossa.

For now, the United States ignored British prime minister Winston Churchill's pleas to enter the war. It did, however, help the Atlantic convoys and provide supplies under the Lend-Lease program.

The United States Enters the War

A rescue boat approaches burning US warships on "Battleship Row" after the Japanese attack on Pearl Harbor in Hawaii.

US president Franklin D. Roosevelt had rejected British pleas to join the war, although he sent supplies to help Britain's war effort. Everything changed on December 7, 1941, when Germany's ally, Japan, launched an attack on the US Pacific Fleet.

On a Sunday morning, around 360 warplanes of the Imperial Japanese Navy attacked the US naval base in Pearl Harbor, Hawaii. The surprise strike was intended to stop the US Navy interfering in Japan's planned attacks on British and Dutch territories in Southeast Asia.

At War!

More than 2,300 Americans died in the attacks, and the Pacific Fleet was crippled. The next day, Congress declared war on Japan. As Japan and Germany were allies, Hitler declared war on the United States four days later. The United States was at war in both Asia and Europe.

US WAR LEADER

In 1940 the Democrat Franklin Delano Roosevelt won an unprecedented third term as US president. At the start of the war, he supported the British by supplying them with arms. After the attack on Pearl Harbor, he was central in the alliance fighting the Axis powers. He also planned for postwar life, including the setting up of the United Nations to settle international disputes. He died on April 12, 1945, a month before Germany surrendered.

Franklin D. Roosevelt addresses the joint houses of the US Congress as he declares war on Japan on December 8, 1941.

Allied Plans

The United States was the most powerful industrial nation in the world. But the Allies—the United States, Britain and its empire, and the Soviet Union—faced a problem. Germany occupied most of Europe and North Africa, and Japan had overrun much of Southeast Asia. The Allies needed to decide which enemy to fight first—and how best to strike at either of them.

A British soldier captures a German tank and its crew during the Battle of El Alamein in the Egyptian desert.

Churchill (left), Roosevelt (center) and Stalin met at Yalta in the Crimea region of southern Russia.

At the start of 1942, Winston Churchill and Franklin D. Roosevelt met at a conference code-named Arcadia in Washington, DC. They decided to defeat Germany first before defeating Japan. Eventually that meant Allied armies would have to invade Europe.

North Africa

At a second Washington conference in June 1942, Roosevelt and Churchill agreed to open a second front in North Africa. Capturing North Africa would open a possible route into southern Europe via the Italian island of Sicily.

YALTA CONFERENCE

In February 1945 Roosevelt and Churchill met the Soviet leader Joseph Stalin at Yalta to discuss the defeat of Germany. Stalin pressed the other leaders to launch their invasion of Europe as soon as possible. He wanted it to divert German resources from the Eastern Front, where the Red Army was under great pressure. The leaders also discussed the shape of postwar Europe, but in fact Stalin was planning to take over much of the eastern part of the continent.

Massive Allied LST (Landing Ship, Tank) are shown at Anzio in Italy. Such assault vessels were desperately needed for D-Day.

Turning Point in the Desert

In North Africa, Field Marshal Erwin Rommel was leading his Afrika Korps east toward the Suez Canal, Britain's route to its colony in India. At El Alamein, in the Egyptian desert, the British stopped Rommel on July 1, 1942. It was the Allies' first victory over the Germans. Churchill noted, "Before Alamein we never had a victory. After Alamein we never had a defeat."

US troops joined the British to clear the Germans from North Africa. Now the US Joint Chiefs of Staff wanted to focus resources on a planned invasion of northern Europe, but the Allies invaded Sicily in July 1943. After the island fell, they landed on the "toe" of Italy in September. To get around German defensive lines, the Americans made another landing on the coast at Anzio in January 1944.

Useful Practice

These landings showed the Allies how to coordinate large amphibious operations. They learned about using air, naval, and land forces together. The lessons would be vital when it came to invading France on D-Day.

STALINGRAD

Allied victories in 1943 did not only come in North Africa and Italy. The German 6th Army had besieged the Soviet city of Stalingrad since August 1942. During the bitter winter, a Soviet counterattack trapped the Germans inside the city. After desperate fighting in the ruined city, the whole army surrendered. The defeat was a turning point of the whole war. The Germans began to retreat while the Soviet Red Army pursued them toward Germany itself.

German soldiers retreat through the snow after the defeat at Stalingrad. The battle was the turning point on the Eastern Front.

German Defenses

German troops march past the gigantic fortifications of the Atlantic Wall in France in April 1944, just two months before D-Day.

The Germans knew the Allies would one day cross the English Channel to try to recapture Europe. They built a system of coastal defenses that ran from Norway to Spain. The huge defenses along the French, Belgian, and Dutch coasts facing the channel were known as the Atlantic Wall.

In January 1944 Field Marshal Erwin Rommel took charge of the defenses and ordered them to be strengthened. Concrete gun emplacements were built along the coast. Barbed wire and other obstacles were piled on the beaches. Millions of mines were laid at sea.

Where Will They Land?

The problem for the Germans was which part of the channel to concentrate on. Hitler believed the Allies would target the Pas-de-Calais region, near the northern French border with Belgium. His commanders were not so sure.

ERWIN ROMMEL

Rommel had served as a Panzer commander during the fall of France and had led the Afrika Korps in North Africa. Hitler made Rommel a field marshal and asked him to reinforce the defenses along the French coast. Rommel disagreed with his superiors about the best way to prevent an invasion. The disagreement meant the Normandy coastal defenses were weaker than they should have been. Implicated in a plot to kill Hitler, Rommel committed suicide in 1944.

The Germans built huge guns along the coast of the Pas-de-Calais region, where Hitler believed the Allies would attempt to land.

Allied Buildup

D-Day was planned for May 1944. That would give the Allies time to open other theaters of the war to stretch the German forces by making them fight on different fronts. It would also give US industry time to manufacture the huge amount of military hardware needed for the invasion.

US soldiers work out on a dock during the buildup to D-Day. Some 75,000 US troops arrived in Britain ready for the landings.

Hundreds of Allied tanks and other vehicles are stockpiled ready to be deployed during the invasion of France.

From 1943 hundreds of thousands of US troops arrived in Britain. Beaches in southern England were similar to those in France, so they were used to practice amphibious landings. Civilians were banned from the coast to keep the preparations secret. However, although thousands of ships and landing craft were requisitioned for use, there were still not enough by May 1944. The landings were put back one month.

Deceiving Hitler

As the invasion came closer, the Allies carried out a large-scale deception exercise. They managed to convince the Germans that the invasion would come near Calais. The deception was easier because Hitler already expected the invasion to come there.

TRAGIC REHEARSAL

In April and May 1944, the Allies carried out full-scale live-fire invasion rehearsals at Slapton Sands in Devon on the English coast. One rehearsal, Operation Tiger, turned into a tragedy when German E-boats attacked the landing craft. The attack was made worse by poor Allied command and communications. In all, 946 US servicemen died. Since the rehearsals were carried out in great secrecy, the disaster was quietly forgotten. The full story only became known after the end of the war.

Setting the Date

SHAEF (Supreme Headquarters Allied Expeditionary Force) planned D-Day under the command of Eisenhower (front, center).

The commander of the invasion was the US general Dwight D. Eisenhower. He had to decide the precise timing of the operation, which was code-named Overlord. Eisenhower needed good weather for the channel crossing and high tides for the landings. He had only a brief period when they would both coincide.

French Resistance fighters prepare for the sabotage campaign against the Germans after hearing secret messages from the BBC.

There were only three days each month when high tides in Normandy would give troops time to get ashore. Winds needed to be light so that landing craft were not swamped in the surf. Cloud cover could be no more than 60 percent so bombers could see their targets.

A Final Delay

Eisenhower got a long-range weather forecast and ordered preparations to begin on May 29. By June 3 the weather had deteriorated so badly that he ordered a 24-hour delay. Then the US Army meteorologist predicted there would be a 24-hour window of better weather from the afternoon of June 5. Eisenhower consulted his senior generals and made the decision to go ahead. June 6 would be D-Day.

FRENCH RESISTANCE

On the evening of June 5, 1944, the BBC in London broadcast a line from a poem by the French poet Paul Verlaine. This was a secret message to the French Resistance that the Allied invasion would begin within 48 hours, and that they should start sabotage raids against the Germans. The Resistance carried out hundreds of sabotage operations against power lines, transportation facilities, and communications networks to isolate the Germans in Normandy before the landings got underway.

Air Landings

With the invasion force at sea in the channel, the last Allied forces to leave for Normandy on June 5 were British and US paratroopers. They were the first to arrive in occupied Europe. Their job was to secure the flanks of the invasion zone to prevent any German counterattack. They were also to capture and hold key bridges and road junctions.

Dozens of Allied gliders lie abandoned in fields behind the beaches. Many gliders crashed on landing.

In the early hours of June 6, 13,000 Allied troops parachuted into Normandy. Another 4,000 landed in 500 gliders. The US 82nd and 101st Airborne Divisions landed behind Utah Beach to seize routes heading inland.

The Plan Goes Wrong

Under heavy fire from German defenders, many pilots dropped their men far from the planned landing zones. Scattered across the countryside, the paratroopers took time to organize themselves. Many staggered around looking for their comrades and skirmishing with the enemy.

SCREAMING EAGLES

Formed at the end of World War I, the 101st Airborne—nicknamed the "Screaming Eagles"—were a parachute and glider regiment trained for air-assault operations. The 101st Airborne played a major role on D-Day, even though they missed many of their landing zones. Later in the war, they played a prominent role in the Battle of the Bulge around Bastogne in Belgium.

Paratroopers of the US 101st Airborne Division board their airplane in England on June 5 ready to jump over France.

Toward the Beaches

As the air attack began, vast numbers of vessels were crossing the English Channel. Smaller ships left ports all over southern England at different times because of the different distances they had to cover. The smaller ships were protected by warships, while fighter planes took to the skies to protect the fleets.

Allied ships head for France across the English Channel. Each has a barrage balloon overhead to discourage dive-bombing.

US landing craft and DUKW amphibious vehicles carry supplies toward the beaches just hours after the first assault waves.

The Allies used destroyers, antisubmarine air patrols, and minefields to seal off the eastern and western approaches to the channel. Meanwhile the invasion vessels assembled and sailed toward Normandy through a channel that had been swept clear of enemy mines.

A Safe Passage

Off the French coast, the fleet split into two task forces. Warships bombarded German positions on the coast while five groups of assault craft positioned for the final push to the beaches. Meticulous planning had got the ships to the right place at the right time.

THE FUNNIES

The larger landing craft carried the "Funnies." These specialized British tanks got their name from their odd attachments. Some carried folding box-girder bridges. Others were fitted with rotating chains to smash through minefields. The Funnies included the amphibious Duplex Drive (DD) Sherman tank. It had twin propellers and a waterproof screen around the hull. It could sail ashore and then drive on its caterpillar tracks, as normal.

Utah Beach

The landings at Utah Beach were the most successful of D-Day. Utah was the furthest west of the landing beaches. It was chosen because it would put the US VII Corps within 40 miles (64 km) of Cherbourg. Control of this major port was essential to allow the Allies to land enough men and supplies to support the invasion.

US troops wade through the surf on their way to Utah Beach. The landings met only light resistance from the Germans.

Bombs from a B-25 Mitchell bomber detonate at a steelworks during the Allied campaign to capture the town of Caen in Normandy.

The naval and air bombardment had cleared many enemy minefields on the beach, although it had caused little damage to German enemy positions. The main obstacles facing the Allies were not the beach defenses but flooded terrain blocking the way inland.

Lucky Break

As the first landing craft approached Utah Beach at 6:30 A.M., strong currents swept them south. They hit the shore 2,000 yards (1,830 m) from their planned landing zone. Luckily for the US infantrymen, the beach there was more lightly defended than the original zone.

AIR COVER

During the build-up to D-Day, the Allies had attacked many German airfields. That left the Luftwaffe severely disadvantaged as British Spitfires and US Lightnings and Mustangs patrolled the skies. Spitfires flew cover and US Thunderbolts and British Typhoon fighter-bombers attacked German targets and reinforcements on the ground. They tried to destroy German aircraft before they had a chance to take off. Only two German airplanes reached the beaches on D-Day.

Only one US general landed on D-Day itself. Brigadier General Theodore Roosevelt Jr., son of former president Theodore Roosevelt, landed with the first wave on Utah Beach. On seeing the situation, he quickly decided to make this new location the landing site.

A Wise Decision

Roosevelt's decision paid off. Not only was the beach less heavily defended, the waters were also calmer. That helped 28 out of the 32 amphibious tanks make it ashore. However, they were not really needed. In less than an hour Roosevelt's men had cleared the beach of Germans.

An Allied rocket ship fires a barrage of high-explosive shells onto German positions to support the landings on Utah Beach.

Among the reporters who landed on D-Day were the author Ernest Hemingway (right) and the photographer Robert Capa (left).

REPORTERS

News of D-Day traveled fast. Many war reporters and photographers sailed with the invasion forces to report firsthand on the day's action. Their reports and images filled the front pages. The US author Ernest Hemingway landed on Omaha Beach with the seventh wave. Hemingway's wife, Martha Gellhorn, and the veteran reporter Virginia Cowles also reported from the front line. The photographer Robert Capa captured iconic images of US soldiers wading ashore under fire on Omaha Beach.

By 9:30 A.M. men and equipment were moving inland. Before noon, the US 4th Division had made contact with the airborne forces who had landed behind the beach.

A Good Day

By nightfall the men from Utah Beach had moved 4 miles (6.4 km) inland. They had suffered only 200 casualties. Utah Beach was a major success: partly because of the thorough planning but partly because of simple luck.

Omaha Beach

US assault troops huddle behind the ramp of their landing craft. Ahead of them, disaster is already unfolding on the beach.

Unlike Utah Beach, the US landings at Omaha Beach were a disaster. The naval and air bombardment had not destroyed the defenses. As the landing craft lowered their ramps, every German gun on the beach opened fire. Many US infantrymen were killed before they could leave their landing craft.

The 1st and 29th Infantry Divisions landed on a wide sandy beach overlooked by tall cliffs. It was an obvious landing point for an invasion, so the Germans had defended it well, with huge gun emplacements on the cliffs.

Disaster

Enemy guns were not the only problems. The sea was rough, and a dozen landing craft sank. Others were pulled off course. Most of the amphibious tanks intended to clear the beach also sank. The air and sea bombardment had missed the beach completely.

POINTE DU HOC

The 2nd Rangers Battalion had the task of destroying a German 155mm gun emplacement on Pointe du Hoc, a cliff overlooking the beach. Using grapple hooks and tubular ladders, they scaled the cliff in just 15 minutes but found the guns had been removed. Eventually a Ranger patrol found five of them in an orchard 1 mile (1.6 km) away and destroyed them. The action is one of the most famous in US Army Ranger history.

US Army Rangers use ropes and tubular ladders to scale the cliff at Pointe du Hoc, just west of the Omaha beachhead.

At 6:30 A.M., as the first craft opened their ramps, the German defenders opened fire. Many troops were killed on the landing craft or drowned when they jumped into deep water. Those who got ashore were shell-shocked and missing their equipment. After two hours, not one man had made it off the beach.

Moving Off the Beach

Organization was slowly restored. Small groups of men began to advance. Colonel George Taylor, commander of the 16th Infantry, told the soldiers with him, "There

Wounded men from 3rd Battalion, 16th Infantry Regiment, shelter from enemy fire under the cliffs at Omaha Beach.

In this famous image of D-Day, men of the US 2nd Infantry Division make their way inland after Omaha Beach has been cleared.

are two kinds of people on this beach: the dead and those about to die." He ordered his men to get moving. By late morning, the first men were starting to fight their way off the beach. Navy destroyers moved close to the shore to shell the German positions.

Breaking Out

By late afternoon, the Americans had pushed over a mile (1.6 km) inland. They were far short of their objectives, however. Omaha had suffered the largest loss of life of any of the beaches. One out of every 19 men who landed was either dead or wounded.

LEAVING THE BEACH

The Americans hoped to move large numbers of troops off Omaha. Instead the breakthrough was achieved by small groups of men who improvised their tactics. They cut paths through barbed wire and minefields, and knocked out strongpoints at close range as they inched up the cliffs. By the end of the day, US troops had two isolated footholds that enabled troops to leave the beach. They were enough to let the Americans exploit weaker German defenses further inland.

Germany Fights Back

As the Americans landed at Utah and Omaha, British and other Allied troops also gained toeholds on three more beaches: Gold, Juno, and Sword. By the end of D-Day, however, the Allies had not moved far inland. They awaited an inevitable German counterattack—but it never came.

Most German tanks in Normandy at the time of D-Day were Panzer Mk IVs, which were a formidable foe for the Allied tanks.

This German gun position is well camouflaged because the Allies' control of the skies made such positions vulnerable to air attack.

The landings took the Germans by surprise. Hitler's tank reserves were positioned to face an invasion near Calais. Resistance sabotage slowed German communications, so other reserves were also slow to arrive.

Heavy Resistance

The Germans already in Normandy fought strongly, however. The Allies suffered heavy casualties as they pushed inland. The US push to the port at Cherbourg faced heavy German resistance. To the east, the Allies had planned to seize the town of Caen on D-Day. Instead, it took weeks before they were able to capture it.

THE GERMAN PANZERS

When the German tank reserves finally reached Normandy, they were very effective. The German Panzers were superior to Allied tanks in firepower and armor. Allied shells often bounced off German Panthers and Tigers, but a hit from a Panzer on an Allied Sherman, Churchill, or Cromwell tank was usually fatal. In a battle at Villers-Bocage on June 13, a German Tiger commanded by Michael Wittmann single-handedly destroyed 11 Allied tanks and 15 other vehicles.

Breakout from Normandy

Weeks of heavy fighting left the town of Caen in ruins. Caen was the center of transportation routes on the Normandy peninsula.

Normandy proved harder to capture than the Allies had planned. After several weeks of bitter fighting, the Allies were still bogged down in the rural landscape of small fields separated by deep lanes and thick hedgerows. The vital town of Caen had still to be taken in the face of growing opposition.

The Allies began an operation code-named Cobra. The British and Canadians would attack Caen while the Americans advanced from the west to encircle the Germans inside the town.

Operation Cobra

On July 25 an air bombardment began the attack. The Allies made quick progress and defeated a German counterattack on August 7. The US advance swung toward Caen, but the Germans escaped the trap. They suffered many casualties, however, and lost much of their equipment. On August 16 Hitler ordered a withdrawal from Normandy.

BOCAGE COUNTRY

Much of the fighting in Normandy took place in a landscape of tiny fields known as the Bocage. This maze of thick hedgerows, tiny roads, and banks of earth up to 10 feet (3 m) high was excellent defensive terrain for the Germans. They fought for every field. The Allies fitted tanks with steel blades to crash through the undergrowth, but the fighting was slow and casualties were high. It took several weeks of heavy fighting before the Allies finally fought their way out of the Bocage.

On the lookout for enemy snipers, US soldiers move carefully along a lane in the Bocage region of Normandy.

Campaign to the Rhine

By the end of the summer of 1944, it seemed as though the war would soon end. The German army was on the verge of collapse as the Allies broke out of Normandy and raced to liberate Paris. They then began to advance toward Germany itself. But the Germans regrouped and fought back. The war had another year to go.

British paratroopers take cover during the airborne assault on Arnhem in the Netherlands during "Operation Market Garden."

British paratroopers are taken prisoner at the end of Market Garden, after Allied armor failed to advance to relieve them.

The Allies freed Paris on August 25. After the slow progress through Normandy, Allied troops now sped through northern France, meeting little opposition. By the end of August, two million Allied soldiers were in France. By early September, the Allies had captured Brussels and Antwerp in Belgium, while Allied troops also landed in the south of France.

Advance Halted

Allied victory seemed just days away. The advance soon stalled, however, as the Germans regrouped. In the north, the British failure to secure the area around Antwerp meant they did not control a port. Instead, supplies had to be landed at the D-Day beaches and driven overland, slowing the process down.

MARKET GARDEN

In September 1944 the Allies devised a daring plan to clear a route through the occupied Netherlands into Germany. Paratroopers were to seize a line of river and canal crossings, including the bridge over the Rhine River at Arnhem. Allied armor would then speed along this route to capture the important German industrial area of the Ruhr. However, opposition from German armor meant Allied ground forces failed to reach the airborne troops at Arnhem. Operation Market Garden had failed.

Further south, the Allies set foot on German soil for the first time on September 11, but were soon pushed back. Even further to the south, the advance of the US 3rd Army was halted when it ran out of fuel.

Toward Germany

During the fall, the Allies marched across France and the Low Countries in heavy rain. They finally captured the Scheldt estuary, which allowed them to use the port at Antwerp. Now they could begin to amass the huge supplies needed for an invasion of Germany. But although the Allies were close to the border along a front that stretched from Belgium almost to Switzerland, it was becoming clear that the Germans were not about to surrender.

Soldiers from the US Seventh Army leave their assault craft under enemy fire as they cross the Rhine on March 26, 1944.

A US soldier looks over the bridge at Remagen. Crossing the Rhine was a logistical problem for the Allies, rather than a military one.

The Battle of the Bulge

The Allies launched advances toward the Ruhr in the north and Frankfurt in the south. But on December 16 the Germans began a shock attack through the dense Ardennes forest between the Allied fronts. The Germans pushed 60 miles (96 km) through Allied lines before finally losing the Battle of the Bulge before Christmas. The Ardennes offensive was Germany's last chance. With Russian troops attacking Germany from the east, the Allies in the west were ready to cross the Rhine into Germany in March 1945.

BRIDGE AT REMAGEN

Adolf Hitler had ordered all bridges across the Rhine to be destroyed to stop the Allied advance. At Remagen, however, troops of the US 1st Army arrived as German engineers were preparing to blow up a railroad bridge on March 7, 1945. They seized the bridge and used it to secure a toehold on the opposite bank. The Germans desperately tried to destroy the bridge, but it was not until ten days later that it collapsed into the river, having been weakened in the fighting.

Allied Victory

A Red Army soldier waves a Soviet flag over the Chancellery in Berlin after the Russian capture of the city on May 7, 1945.

The western Allies crossed the Rhine on March 24 and pushed into the heart of Germany. As the Red Army approached Berlin from the east, it was clear that the war would soon be over. The Germans, however, continued to fight on to defend their homeland.

In mid-April the western Allies surrounded and captured German Army Group B. The Allies crossed Germany and met up with the Russians on April 24 at Torgau on the Elbe River. But Eisenhower now halted the advance. The Allied leaders had agreed that the Russians alone would have the task of taking Berlin.

Boy Soldiers

The Germans were so short of troops that boys as young as 10 and 11 were pressed into service. In April 1945 some 5,000 boys joined the fight against the Red Army in Berlin. Adolf Hitler committed suicide on April 30 while the battle raged in the city's streets. On May 7, 1945, Germany finally surrendered. Nazi rule was over.

DEATH OF HITLER

Adolf Hitler spent his last months in an air-raid shelter near the Chancellery in Berlin. From his bunker, he conducted a desperate bid to stop the Allied advances. Eventually he realized that defeat was inevitable. On April 29 he married his long-term girlfriend, Eva Braun. The next day, Hitler shot himself and Braun took poison. His bodyguards then burned the bodies.

In the last photograph ever taken of Adolf Hitler, the German leader hands out medals to young soldiers in Berlin in April 1945.

TIMELINE

1939 September 1: German troops invade Poland, beginning World War II.

1940 May 10: German forces invade Belgium, the Netherlands, and Luxembourg, beginning the war on the Western Front.
June 22: France surrenders to Germany.
July–August: In the Battle of Britain, the German Luftwaffe fail to defeat the RAF to open the way for an invasion of Britain.
September 7: German bombers begin the nightly raids on British cities known as the Blitz.

1941 February: German troops arrive in North Africa to help their Italian allies fight the British.
June 22: Hitler launches Operation Barbarossa, when more than 3 million troops invade the Soviet Union.
December 7: Japanese aircraft bomb the US naval base at Pearl Harbor in Hawaii.
December 8: The United States declares war on Japan.
December 12: Adolf Hitler declares war on the United States.

1942 January: President Roosevelt and British prime minister Winston Churchill agree to defeat Germany before tackling Japan. Plans for an Allied landing in northern Europe begin.
July: In North Africa, British troops defeat the Germans for the first time at the Battle of El Alamein.
November 8: US troops arrive in North Africa.

1943 February 2: A Soviet counteroffensive lifts the siege of Stalingrad, turning the tide of the war on the Eastern Front.
July 10: British and US troops invade Sicily.
September 3: Allied troops invade mainland Italy.

1944 January 22: US troops stage a large-scale amphibious landing at Anzio in Italy.
April: Full-scale rehearsals for D-Day begin on the southern coast of Britain.
June 4: The Allied Supreme Commander, General Dwight D. Eisenhower, confirms D-Day as June 6.
June 5: The BBC broadcasts secret messages telling the French Resistance to begin a sabotage campaign against German communications.
June 6: D-Day. Thousands of Allied paratroopers and glider troops land in Normandy before dawn. From around 6:30 A.M. thousands more troops land on five beaches. By nightfall some 160,000 Allied troops have come ashore.
July 25: After weeks of fighting, the Allies begin Operation Cobra, the breakout from Normandy.
August 25: Allied troops liberate Paris.
September: Operation Market Garden, an Allied thrust into the Netherlands, fails to break through to Germany.
December 16: A German attack through the Ardennes begins the Battle of the Bulge, but the Germans are defeated before Christmas.

1945 March 7: US soldiers seize an intact bridge across the Rhine at Remagen.
March 24: US troops cross the Rhine.
April 24: Allied troops meet Soviet troops advancing from the east at the Elbe River, where the Allied advance halts.
April 30: With Red Army troops fighting in the streets of Berlin, Adolf Hitler commits suicide in his bunker.
May 7: Germany surrenders, ending World War II in Europe.

GLOSSARY

air superiority A situation in which one air force makes it too dangerous for enemy planes to fly.

amphibious An operation that takes place on land and at sea.

armor Armored vehicles, such as tanks or personnel carriers.

Axis The name given to the alliance of Germany, Italy, and Japan.

BBC British Broadcasting Corporation, the national TV and radio station in Britain.

gliders Aircraft without engines that fly by using thermal currents in the air.

infantry Soldiers who are trained and armed to fight on foot.

landing craft Flat-bottomed boats with ramps used to carry troops and equipment onto beaches.

Lend-Lease Act A US government program that allowed the Allies to buy war equipment on credit.

mines Bombs laid at sea or buried in the ground that explode when something touches them.

Panzer The German name for a tank.

paratroopers Soldiers who are trained to parachute into action.

requisitioned Describes something that is temporarily taken over for military use.

Resistance A French organization set up to fight German occupation through acts such as sabotage.

sabotage Destroying equipment and transportation networks to disrupt enemy operations.

stockpile To gather together stores for an operation.

strategic Something that is related to an overall conflict, rather than to a short-term victory in a battle.

theater A major region in which a distinct part of a war is fought.

FURTHER INFORMATION

Books

Connolly, Sean. *The D-Day Landings* (Witness to History). Heinemann-Raintree, 2008.

Davenport, John C. *D-Day and the Liberation of France* (Milestones in Modern World History). Chelsea House Publications, 2010.

Martin, Martha. *D-Day* (Crabtree Chrome). Crabtree Publishing Company, 2012.

Miller, Terry. *D-Day: The Allies Strike Back During World War II* (24/7 Goes to War: On the Battlefield). Scholastic Library Publishing, 2009.

Murray, Doug. *D-Day: The Liberation of Europe Begins*. Rosen Publishing Group, 2008.

Vasant, Wayne. *Normandy: A Graphic History of D-Day, The Allied Invasion of Hitler's Fortress Europe*. Zenith Press, 2012.

Websites

www.pbs.org/wgbh/amex/dday/
Online companion to the PBS series *American Experience*.

www.army.mil/d-day/
US Army site dedicated to D-Day, with photographs and accounts.

www.dday.org/
National D-Day Memorial site, with a complete account of US participation in the landings.

www.dday.co.uk
The Normandy beaches as they are today.

Publisher's note to educators and parents: Our editors have carefully reviewed these websites to ensure that they are suitable for students. Many websites change frequently, however, and we cannot guarantee that a site's future contents will continue to meet our high standards of quality and educational value. Be advised that students should be closely supervised whenever they access the Internet.

INDEX